W9-ABA-677

Make a

Powered Boat

by Meg Gaertner

NORWOOD HOUSE PRESS

Norwood House Press
P.O. Box 316598
Chicago, Illinois 60631

For information regarding Norwood House Press, please visit our website at:
www.norwoodhousepress.com or call 866-565-2900.

LIBRARY OF CONGRESS CATALOGING-IN-PUBLICATION DATA

Names: Gaertner, Meg, author.
Title: Make a powered boat / by Meg Gaertner.
Description: Chicago, Illinois : Norwood House Press, [2018] | Series: Make your own: make it go! | Includes bibliographical
    references and index.
Identifiers: LCCN 2018007289 (print) | LCCN 2018008509 (ebook) | ISBN 9781684041961 (ebook) | ISBN 9781599539249 (hardcover
    : alk. paper)
Subjects: LCSH: Boats and boating--Design and construction—Juvenile literature. | Boats and boating--Models--Juvenile literature.
Classification: LCC GV775.3 (ebook) | LCC GV775.3 .G34 2018 (print) | DDC 623.82--dc23
LC record available at https://lccn.loc.gov/2018007289

312N—072018
Manufactured in the United States of America in North Mankato, Minnesota.

Contents

CHAPTER 1

The speed of a boat is measured in knots.

All about Boats

Humans have been traveling in boats for tens of thousands of years. Boats must be big enough to carry many people and objects across the water. Their large size makes them very heavy. But boats can still float on water despite their weight. Using common household items, you can make a powered boat that will help you understand how full-size boats work.

When an object is put in water, it pushes water out of the way. The object makes room for itself. This is called **displacement**. For example, take a glass of water. Drop an ice cube into the glass. Did the water level rise? This is an example of displacement!

But this does not explain why some objects float and other objects sink. Two **forces** act on things that are in water. **Gravity** is a force that pulls everything toward the center of the earth. **Buoyancy** pushes objects up. Buoyancy has to do with the weight of the fluid displaced by the object. An object floats if gravity pulls on it less than buoyancy pushes it up. If you make your boat with the right materials, it will be buoyant like a life-size boat.

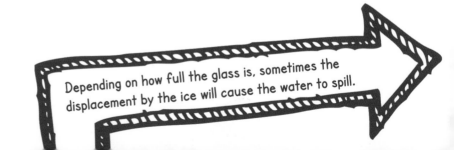

Depending on how full the glass is, sometimes the displacement by the ice will cause the water to spill.

Imagine a rock the size of your fist. The rock is heavy. It is also small, and it does not displace a lot of water. This is because of its compact and dense shape. The rock sinks because it is heavier than the water it displaces. Now imagine a boat. The boat is very large and heavy. But it also displaces a lot of water. The water that it displaces weighs even more than the boat itself. This is because boats are not solid all the way through. Boats have many hollow spaces for storing items and carrying people. Because the boat is less heavy than the water it displaces, the boat is able to float on top of the water.

Sails direct the wind best when they are shaped like a triangle.

Once a boat can float, there are different ways to make it move. Some boats have sails that catch the wind. The wind pushes the boat forward. Other boats have motors that are similar to engines in cars. The motors burn fuel to make the boat move. Your powered boat won't use wind or motors. Instead, it will use a **chemical reaction** to help make it move.

Parts of a Sailboat

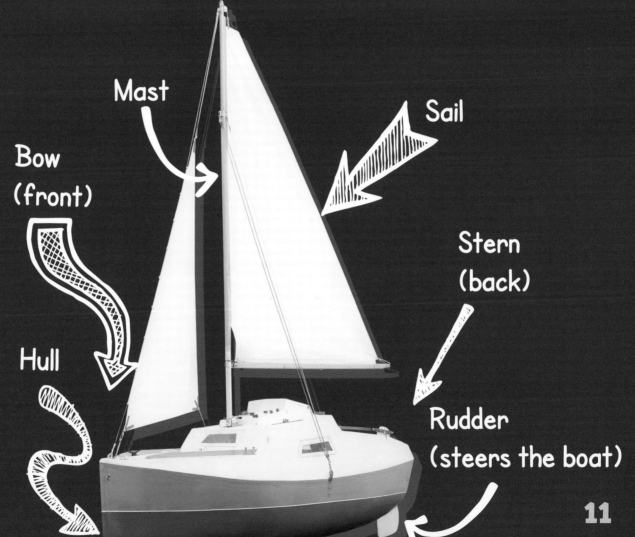

Mast

Sail

Bow
(front)

Stern
(back)

Hull

Rudder
(steers the boat)

11

Some powered boats aren't made to be fast.

CHAPTER 2

Making a Powered Boat

A powered boat needs a body, which is also called the hull.
The body of your boat must be light enough to float. Cardboard
might work, but cardboard gets soft and soggy in water.
The boat must be made of a material that is not harmed by
water. Styrofoam is a good option. It is made to resist water.
Many boats come to a point at their front rather than end in

a flat edge. This shape helps the boat cut through the water and move quickly.

Your boat also needs an engine. This will make the boat move. This engine will be different from engines in full-size boats. In your boat, the engine will be the place where the chemical reaction happens. The engine needs to be small and light so it will not weigh the boat down. A plastic lid, such as a lid from a juice bottle or milk jug, will work.

The lid must be secured to the boat. Both tape and glue can be used to connect the lid to the boat. But some types of tape and glue do not last in water. Duct tape is a type of tape that resists water. It will last longer in water than other kinds of tape.

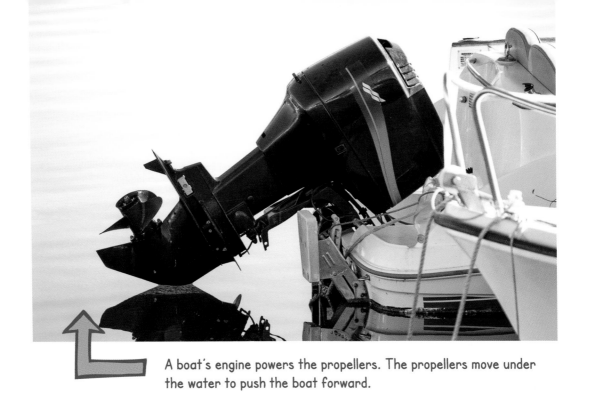

A boat's engine powers the propellers. The propellers move under the water to push the boat forward.

Once you have built your boat, it is time to create the chemical reaction to power your boat. This will happen by mixing baking soda and vinegar in your engine. Your boat will move because of the movement of **atoms**. Atoms are the smallest pieces of matter

The motor from a powered boat creates bubbles in the water similar to the bubbles from a chemical reaction.

that anything can be broken into. Atoms come together in groups called **molecules**.

A chemical reaction occurs when two or more kinds of molecules interact. For example, when an **acid** and a **base** mix, they create a chemical reaction. Vinegar is an acid. Baking soda is a base. Two things happen when you mix baking soda and vinegar in the engine of your boat. First the baking soda and vinegar molecules trade atoms. They combine to create two new molecules. These molecules are called sodium acetate and carbonic acid. Then the carbonic acid breaks down. Atoms in the carbonic acid molecule separate into two groups.

One group forms to make water. The other group of atoms becomes a gas called **carbon dioxide**. The gas escapes into the air. This will be what makes your boat move.

How the boat moves depends on where that gas goes. For the boat to move forward, the gas must be directed backward. This is because of the **Third Law of Motion**. This law says that for every action there is an equal and opposite reaction.

Imagine you are running down the street. You press against the ground with your feet. You push the ground away from you and behind you with a certain amount of force. This motion sends you forward with the same amount of force. This kind of force is what will power the boat. The force of the escaping gas pushes the boat forward.

But how do you control where the gas goes? In this activity, you can use straws to direct the gas behind the boat. To make a powered boat, first make the shape of the boat. Then make the engine. Finally, add the baking soda and vinegar. Watch the boat go!

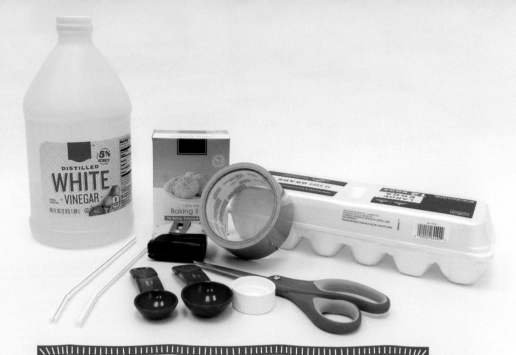

Materials Checklist

✓ Styrofoam egg carton

✓ Scissors

✓ Tape measure

✓ Tablespoons

✓ Plastic lid (from a

juice bottle or milk jug)

✓ Duct tape

✓ 2 plastic bendable straws

✓ Baking soda

✓ Vinegar

19

Styrofoam egg cartons are very buoyant.

CHAPTER 3

Make It Go!

Now that you know how powered boats work, let's put our knowledge to use and build one!

1. Cut a large rectangle out of the egg carton. Then cut the top of your rectangle at an angle on both the left and ride side. This will form a tip for the front of your boat.

2. Place the plastic lid on the boat. Place it flat side down so it forms a small bowl shape. The lid should be closer to the back end.

3. Tape the plastic lid to the boat. Be sure to not cover the entire lid.

4. Next, cut the straws. They should each be about 4 inches (10 cm) long. You will use the bendy parts of the straws.

5. Place the straws side-by-side in the lid. They should point toward the back of the boat. Make sure they stick to the tape.

6. Fill the lid with ½ tablespoon of baking soda.

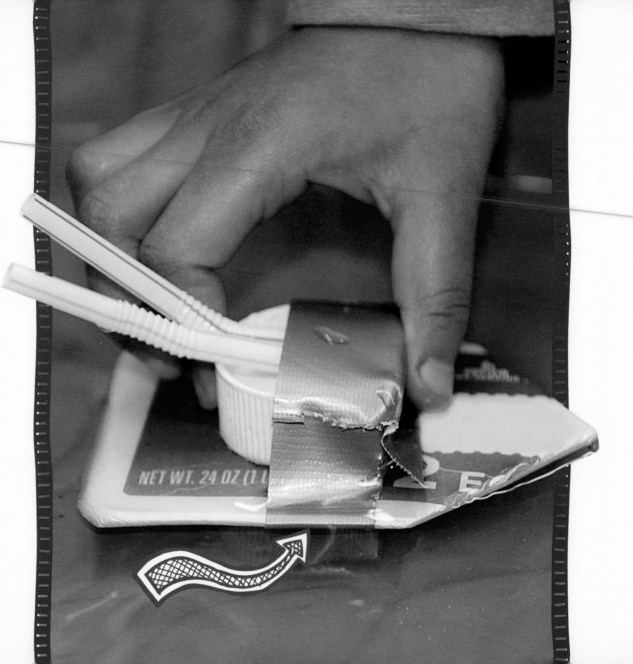

7. Place the boat in the water. You can use a bathtub filled with water. You can also use a kiddie pool outside.

8. Pour 1 tablespoon of vinegar into the plastic lid. Watch the boat go!

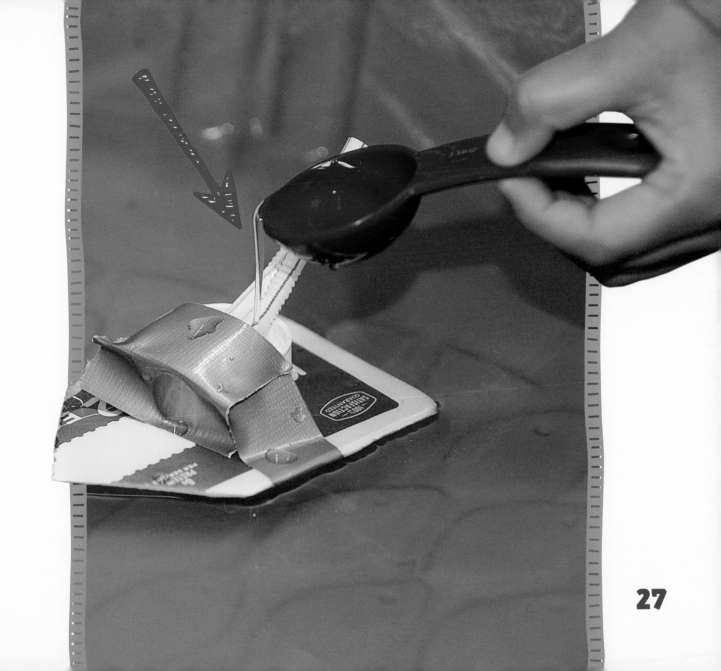

9. Note: Do you see bubbles following the boat as it moves? Those

bubbles are carbon dioxide gas.

Make It Better!

Congratulations! You built a powered boat. Now see if there are ways to improve it. Use any of these changes and see how they improve your powered boat.

- This boat used Styrofoam because it is light. Styrofoam also holds up in water. What else could be used to make the boat that could make it move farther or faster?

- Plastic lids come in many sizes. Does changing the size of the lid change how fast the boat moves?

- The straws direct the carbon dioxide gas to the back of the boat. Does changing the length of the straws change how the boat moves?

Can you think of any ways that you could improve or change your powered boat to work better?

Glossary

acid (ASS-id): A sour substance that can break down metals.

atoms (AT-uhms): The smallest pieces of an element that can exist alone or in a combination.

base (BAYSS): A bitter-tasting component that is capable of mixing with an acid.

buoyancy (BOI-uhn-see): The force that pushes up objects in water.

carbon dioxide (KAR-buhn dye-OK-side): A colorless, odorless gas that forms when a carbonic acid and a base mix, such as baking soda and vinegar.

chemical reaction (KEM-uh-kuhl ree-AK-shuhn): A chemical change when two or more substances combine to make a new substance.

displacement (diss-PLAYSS-ment): The action by which an object pushes water out of the way to make room for itself.

forces (FOHRS-iz): The interactions that change the motion of an object.

gravity (GRAV-uh-tee): The force that pulls everything toward the center of the earth.

molecules (MOL-uh-kyoolz): Groups of atoms.

Third Law of Motion (THURD LAW uhv MOH-shuhn): The law that states for every action there is an equal and opposite reaction.

For More Information

Books

Janet Slingerland, *Explore Atoms and Molecules!* White River Junction, VT: Nomad, 2017. This book includes 25 projects to help students explore atoms, molecules, and chemical reactions.

Justine Ciovacco, *All about Small Boats.* New York: Britannica Educational Publishing, 2017. Students explore how boats float and move in this book about the structure and uses of small boats throughout history.

Science Encyclopedia: Atom Smashing, Food Chemistry, Animals, Space, and More! Washington, DC: National Geographic, 2016. This reference book includes weird but true facts, statistics, and do-it-yourself experiments.

Websites

PBS Kids: Build Watercraft (pbskids.org/designsquad/build/watercraft) Students test their engineering skills as they design and create a floating boat in this activity.

PBS Kids: Soda Bottle Boat (pbskids.org/zoom/activities/sci/sodabottleboat.html) Students learn another way of using a baking soda and vinegar reaction to make a powered boat.

Scholastic Study Jams!: Atoms: Protons, Neutrons, Electrons (studyjams.scholastic.com/studyjams/jams/science/matter/atoms.htm) Students learn about the building blocks of atoms in this article.

Index

About the Author

Meg Gaertner is a children's book author and editor who lives in Minnesota. When not writing, she enjoys dancing and spending time outdoors.